THE EAST INDIA COMPANY
BOOK OF
COFFEE

ANTONY WILD

THE EAST INDIA COMPANY

BOOK OF

COFFEE

ANTONY WILD

HarperCollins*Publishers*

First published in 1994 by
HarperCollins*Publishers*, London

Reprinted 1994

Text © Antony Victor Wild

Antony Wild asserts the moral right to
be identified as the author of this work

Commissioning Editor: Polly Powell
Editor: Lisa Eaton
Cover Design: Ian Butterworth
Designer: Rachel Smyth
Picture Researcher: Nadine Bazar

The publishers and author would like to thank
David Hutton, Drew Smith, Valerie Light,
Robert Baldwin and Edward Bramah.

**A catalogue record for this book is
available from the British Library**

ISBN 0 00 412 739 0

Colour reproduction by Colourscan, Singapore
Printed and bound in Italy

Contents

The Armorial Bearings of the Company of Merchants of London
trading into the East Indies granted by Garter and Clarenceux
Kings of Arms in 1600 and as borne and used until 1709

*F*ounded by the Royal Charter of Queen Elizabeth I in 1600, the East India Company was the single most powerful economic force that the world has ever seen. Its influence reached out to all continents, and the consequences of its actions, both great and small, are the very fabric of history. The Company created British India; founded Hong Kong and Singapore; caused the Boston Tea Party; employed Captain Kidd to combat piracy; held Napoleon captive; and made the fortune of Elihu Yale who founded his famous university with the proceeds.

The Stars and Stripes was inspired by its flag, its shipyards provided the model for St Petersburg, its London chapel set the pattern for New England churches, its administration still forms the basis of Indian bureaucracy, and its corporate structure was the earliest example of a joint stock company. It introduced tea to Britain and India, woollens to Japan, chintzes to America, spices to the West Indies, opium to China, porcelain to Russia, and polo to Persia. It had its own armies, navies, currencies, and territories as diverse as the tiny Spice Island, Pulo Run – later exchanged for Manhattan

– and the 'Jewel in the Crown', India itself. As *The Times* newspaper reported in 1874 when the Company was finally absorbed by the Crown: 'It is just as well to record that it accomplished a work such as in the whole history of the human race no other Company ever attempted and, as such, is ever likely to attempt in the years to come.'

East India House

The Story of Coffee

Origins

*M*any major discoveries are the inspiration for colourful stories, and coffee is no exception. The keepers of the coffee houses in the Middle East used to employ storytellers to entertain their patrons, and it is easy to imagine that the stories of the discovery of coffee have their origins in these tales.

There is, however, little need for invention, as the history of the spread of coffee drinking is fairly well documented. The story begins in Aden in 1454, when a certain Sheik Gemaleddin, a scholarly Muslim cleric, or Mufti, fell ill. He had once spent many years escaping religious persecution in exile in Ethiopia, where he had observed the custom of crushing the cherries of a wild native bush with animal fat and maize, to make a sustaining foodstuff. In an attempt to cure his illness, he called for the same cherries, and they were so successful that he recommended them to his monks to help keep them awake in their nightly devotions. It was, however, the ruler of neighbouring Mocha at that time, Shadomer Shadli, who was credited with suggesting that the cherries be infused to make a drink. Thus coffee first came to be cultivated in that region, now known as Yemen, and until the 18th century the port of Mocha held an effective monopoly of the world's coffee supplies.

The coffee trade

Coffee had been known throughout Europe since the early years of the 17th century. The adoption of coffee drinking in Vienna led to a slow but gradual acceptance of the new fashion in the higher reaches of the Danube, and eventually to Nuremburg in Germany, where the demand was supplied by Venetian traders. At the the Court of Frederick William, the Great Elector in Berlin, the medicinal qualities of coffee were briefly recognized, but it was not until well into the 18th

Recipe for Peppermint Coffee Crème

Pour 2fl oz (62ml) of crème de menthe into a warmed spirit glass, and add 1 teaspoon of sugar and 8fl oz (250ml) of coffee, stirring well. Pour on double cream, lightly whipped, over a spoon, so that it settles on top of the coffee. Decorate with slithers of mint chocolate and do not stir.

The Legendary Bean

Coffee legends abound, from the story of Kaldi and his dancing goats, to the more exotic tale of Omar and the amazing 'coffeebird', which was very popular a hundred years ago. This is an extremely complicated story, involving ghostly giants, plague-ravaged cities, and beautiful princesses long before the fabulous 'coffeebird' even makes an appearance. The Kaldi legend is much more simple – the tale of a shepherd boy whose goats began to dance after eating coffee cherries – which is probably why it is the one most commonly repeated today.

Black as hell, strong as death, sweet as love.
Turkish proverb

Left: Turkish soldiers drinking coffee together, c. 1820

German coffee server, 1735

century that coffee started to challenge the supremacy of that favourite north German beverage, beer. In France the visit of the Turkish Ambassador, Soliman Aga, to the Court of Louis XIV started a fashion for all things Turkish, including coffee drinking, which only the rich could afford at first, since coffee could be obtained only through Marseilles. By 1672 an enterprising Armenian named Pascal had started a coffee house in the market place of Saint-Germain, decked out in the Turkish style. It was not until 1702, however, that the first really successful coffee house, the Café Procope, was opened in Paris by an Italian, and the future of coffee was assured.

The activities of Dutch traders to and from the East Indies brought Holland into contact with the coffee trade out of Mocha. Although it did not really catch on back in Amsterdam and Rotterdam, it made the perfect cash crop for their new possessions of Java and Sumatra. The British were

slow to join the trend towards coffee drinking, and the first coffee house in London did not open until 1650. However, the East India Company, whose Charter of 1600 gave it a monopoly on trade east of the Cape of Good Hope, were aware that coffee was an important trading commodity in the East, and as early as 1607 had committed ships to visit Aden and adjacent ports to explore the possibilities. Rather than bringing it back to Europe, where there was as yet little demand for coffee, the Company started selling it in Persia and Mogul India. Once the coffee house boom started at the end of the 17th century, however, the East India Company became the largest and most successful importer of coffee for the British market.

17th century London coffee house

A Chequered Past

The spread of coffee over the years has been beset with more than its fair share of villainy and intrigue. It was, in fact, a pilgrim to Mecca, Badu Budan, who smuggled the first coffee plants from Yemen back to his native India – hiding the plants by strapping them to his belly. He planted them outside his cave in Mysore province, south India, where, according to legend, they can still be seen to this day.

After the Dutch had successfully established plantations in Java, they sought to please Louis XIV of France by presenting him with a coffee bush – an act which was to have unforeseen consequences. The King was strangely besotted with the bush, which he kept in

Café Turc, Paris, c. 1810

a greenhouse at Versailles, and he spent hours in silent contemplation of it. An enterprising nobleman, the Duke de Clieu, on leave from his posting on Martinique in the Caribbean, decided that coffee would be ideal for his island, and bribed the head gardener to give him three seedlings. De Clieu's voyage back to Martinique with his plants has become immortalized in French poems and songs. As well as fighting off pirates and surviving storms, de Clieu shared the last of his water ration with the only surviving plant. A fellow passenger, jealous of the attention that the Duke was giving the poor bush, attempted to seize it from him, but managed only to tear off a branch. Undeterred, the Duke fulfilled his dream and brought coffee to Martinique, from where plants were taken throughout the Caribbean.

Less noble is the tale of Don Francisco, sent by the Emperor of Brazil to steal coffee seeds from French Guyana in 1727. The French were guarding their coffee jealously, but Don Francisco was equal to the task. Suave, charming and handsome, he made a great impression on the French Governor's wife, and upon leaving she presented him with a bouquet of flowers, in which were concealed the seedlings he desired. As a result of this affair, the forerunners of the world's biggest coffee plantations were founded in Brazil.

Alexander Pope wrote, 'Coffee, which makes the politician wise, And see through all things with his half-shut eyes.'

Coffee today

From its humble origins in Ethiopia, coffee has grown to become a vast economic and cultural force. The coffee industry is the world's largest in terms of manpower, employing over 25 million people worldwide in its cultivation and production. After oil, it is the world's most traded commodity in terms of value, with over 70 million bags (5 million tons) of coffee bought each year, representing a vital source of income for many Third World countries. The world's heaviest coffee-drinking nation is Finland, where they consume 26½ pounds (12 kilos) of coffee per person per year.

French advertisement, 1922

How Coffee is Produced

Bushes and beans

*A*s coffee began to be consumed throughout the world, inevitably more countries started to grow it, and cultivation spread from the Caribbean to Brazil, which now produces about a third of the world's coffee. The second largest producer is Columbia, whose plantations serve as a useful example of how coffee is produced.

The high mountains of the Central Cordillera provide excellent growing conditions for the best of the coffee plant species, *Coffea arabica (see illustration above)*. The warm tropical climate ensures that there are no damaging frosts, the cloud

Coffee cherries on the bush

and tree cover protects the coffee bush from the blistering sun, and the rich soil provides the necessary nourishment. The altitude also makes the nights cool, slowing the growth of the plants, and allowing the coffee to develop fully its finest flavour.

Five years after the seedlings are planted, the mature coffee plant will start to produce bright red cherries – the coffee bean is the stone of that cherry. Left to its own devices the coffee bush can grow up to 60 feet (18 metres) high, but on plantations is kept to about 8 feet (2.4 metres) to make the picking less hazardous. At any one time a coffee bush may have both ripe red cherries and green unripe cherries, so the bush must be picked many times before the harvest is gathered. As there

Green coffee beans and coffee cherries

is no machine which can distinguish between ripe and unripe cherries, picking cannot be mechanized, and this is one of the reasons why so many people worldwide work as coffee pickers.

After the cherries have been gathered, the stone must be separated from the pulp. This is achieved by soaking the cherries in water and stripping off the pulp with a machine known as a huller. At this point the bean is still surrounded by a thin skin called the parchment. The leftover pulp has no use and is dug back into the ground. The parchment is laid out to dry and any obviously defective beans picked out. The coffee is then put into temporary sacks and taken down to a central processing factory where the farmer is paid for his produce.

Brazilian coffee plantation, 1935

Ship to shore

The coffee sacks are reopened, and the coffee is then put through another machine to strip off the thin parchment skin. The green beans, which eventually form the roasted coffee bean, are revealed, and again sorted thoroughly by hand. In some countries, such as Kenya, this sorting is done by machine. The coffee is now ready to be put into sacks, which are stamped and transported to central warehouses in the ports. Green unroasted coffee can be stored in cool, dry conditions for up to two years; coffee producers have warehousing which meets these requirements, but in the high temperatures and humidity of tropical climates, storage is both difficult and expensive, and ideally the coffee should be shipped as soon as possible to the countries where it is to be consumed.

Modern storage sacks

Nature's Helpers

Some of the world's most expensive and bizarre coffees are not picked by people at all. Take Kopi Luak coffee, for example, a special delicacy in Japan and Sumatra. The luak is a small cat-like creature which likes nothing better than to prowl around a Sumatran coffee plantation at night, selecting the finest, ripest coffee cherries to eat. Naturally it finds the stone of the coffee cherry – the bean – indigestible, and the results are there for all to see the next morning. Fermentation inside the luak's stomach imparts a distinctive and much sought-after taste – full-bodied and very smooth – to the coffee beans after they have been cleaned and roasted. This coffee is particularly valued in Japan, where it fetches enormous prices, as well as being a favourite of the plantation managers and owners. In addition to Kopi Luak, there are coffees which have been similarly treated by monkeys and parrots in India, and there is even a Vietnamese weasel coffee.

Recipe for Iced Coffee

Prepare coffee in the normal way, but a little stronger than usual. Allow to cool, then place in a covered container in the refrigerator until it is no more than 39°F (4°C). If left to stand too long, however, the flavour will deteriorate.

Roasting and blending

A coffee bean is usually one half of the stone of a coffee cherry – the whole stone comprises two beans with flat sides laid face to face. The peaberry bean, which occurs in less than ten per cent of cherries, is a single bean stone. Arabica coffee plants produce a more elongated, flatter bean than the inferior *Coffea robusta* bean.

During roasting, which takes about ten minutes at 425°F (220°C), a series of complex chemical reactions takes place, which develops the characteristic coffee aroma and flavour. Most visible of the results is the change in size of the bean, caused by the expansion of its cell structure, and the change in colour, resulting from the caramelization of sugars and

Hand coffee roaster

other carbohydrates. Inside the bean over 600 different volatile oils form and, although they constitute less than three per cent of the end product by weight, without them coffee would neither smell nor taste of anything. These oils are extremely prone to oxidation, posing a serious problem for the coffee industry, which has devised various methods to try to preserve them. This task is made no easier by the fact that coffee, in the first 48 hours after roasting, gives off six times its volume in carbon dioxide – enough to blow open a pack.

The degree to which the coffee is roasted makes a great difference to the flavour. Sometimes this reflects national or regional habits – southern Italian coffee, for example, is generally roasted darker than northern Italian – or sometimes personal preference. The relationship between colour and taste is a matter of common sense; a light roast tends to leave more of the green, vegetable flavours, whereas in a medium roast, these flavours tend towards acidity, accompanied by a more developed body and a better balanced flavour, which in the dark roasts become more of a bitter, burnt flavour. Whilst there are no fixed rules about what roast is suitable for any particular bean, it would be a shame to inflict a very dark continental roast on a fine gourmet or specialist coffee, as you would taste the roast more than the coffee. The art of coffee roasting lies in determining the exact depth of roast to bring out the best in a particular coffee, allowing the optimum development of flavour, acidity and body.

Keeping coffee fresh

The coffee bean itself can keep in good condition for up to six weeks, as long as it is not ground until immediately before use. Rapid oxidation means that ground coffee has to be packed correctly in order to keep out as much of the harmful oxygen as possible. This can be achieved by vacuum packing, 'gas flushing' with carbon dioxide or nitrogen, or using a valve which allows out the carbon dioxide produced by the coffee, but does not allow oxygen in. Specialist shops resolve the problem by actually roasting coffee in their shops or nearby.

In the home it is possible to slow down the oxidation process, (which makes coffee become stale), by putting the ground coffee or beans in an airtight container in the refrigerator, or, better still, the freezer. A cold temperature slows down the rate of oxidation, and an airtight container protects the coffee from picking up other aromas – something that it is prone to do.

Celebrated Drinkers

Notorious coffee drinkers include Louis XIV of France, Napoleon, J.S.Bach, composer of the Coffee Cantata, *and Gustavus III of Sweden, who, having condemned a pair of twins to death, fed one entirely on tea and the other on coffee, concluding that coffee was healthier because the tea twin died first aged 83. The award for devotion to coffee, however, must be given to the 19th century author Honoré de Balzac. He was one of France's most prolific writers, a feat achieved by drinking over 60 cups of coffee a day and sleeping only two hours a night.*

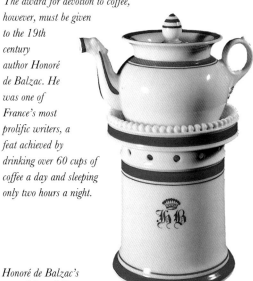

Honoré de Balzac's porcelain cafetière

Varieties of Coffee

Where coffee comes from

*T*he requirements of botany, temperature and altitude mean that the best arabica coffee comes from tropical countries with high plains or mountains, and an adequate water supply. Whilst a country like Brazil produces vast amounts of coffee, it cannot achieve the quality of that produced in Colombia or Kenya, mainly because Brazilian plantations are at less than 3000 feet (915 metres) above sea level. The rapid growth of the coffee plant at such an altitude prohibits the development of the finer notes which distinguish the higher quality coffees. Over 70 countries produce coffee; from Central and South America, the Caribbean, Africa and India, to Java, Sumatra and the Far East.

A considerable quantity of a hardier strain of the coffee plant, robusta, is grown in West African countries such as Cameroon and the Ivory Coast, where the plantations are often almost at sea level. The coarse rubbery-flavoured coffees produced by the robusta bush are considerably cheaper than the fine arabicas, and thus find their way into inferior blends of instant and ground coffee. However, they are also well suited to the espresso method of making coffee, and even the highest quality espresso blends may include some robusta coffees, as they help in the development of the 'cream' – the rich foam on the top of an espresso coffee.

Speciality and blended coffees

Speciality or gourmet coffees are those from a particular estate, area or country, and are of a specially high quality, or have a distinctive and desirable taste. However, just because a coffee comes from Kenya, it does not automatically mean that it has that fruity acidity for which the best Kenyan coffees are prized. Blended coffees can include some of the world's

Brazilian coffee plantation

finest speciality coffees, but more frequently are made from coffee from a mixture of origins. The skill of the blender lies in successfully marrying the various characteristics of the coffees he or she uses, to create a blend in which the whole is better than the sum of the parts.

Recipe for Almond and Coffee Cake

Beat two whites of eggs until they are stiff, then delicately mix a coffee-flavoured crème pâtissière. Add 5oz (150g) of ground almonds, 3½oz (100g) of caster sugar, and 3½oz (100g) of melted butter. Line the walls of a cake tin with sponge fingers and put the mixture in the middle. Allow to cool carefully over a long period before taking out of the tin.

Coffee Tasting Terms

We all have the ability to taste, but simply lack the vocabulary to express what it is that we are tasting. As one acquires the words, one learns to dissect the taste sensation, and to differentiate between the elements that make up a flavour.

Acidity – This describes a pleasant sharpness on the tip of the tongue, akin to that of a dry white wine. It can have a fruity quality, such as in Kenyan coffees, or a metallic quality, such as in those from Mexico.

Body – This describes the illusory sense of weight of a liquid on the tongue; a full-bodied coffee, such as a Java, will feel heavier and richer than a light-bodied one.

Earthy – The heavy, sweet body of Sumatran and Javan coffees can sometimes lapse into an earthy flavour, a rather unpleasant musty taste.

Rioy – Named after Rio de Janeiro in Brazil, this describes the 'hard', medicinal or iodine taste favoured in the eastern Mediterranean.

Gamey – A pleasant curdled flavour, similar to that of yogurt in relation to milk, sometimes apparent in Ethiopian and Arabian coffees.

Rubbery – The distinctive coarse flavour of robusta coffees.

Green – The harsh grassy flavour in coffee which has not fully developed in the roast, or has been incorrectly processed.

Well-balanced – When the qualities of acidity, body and flavour are in harmony, so that no one element predominates at the expense of an other.

Region by region

Latin America

Coffees from this part of the world generally have a fine acidity (which can verge on the metallic), a smooth flavour and a medium body.

Costa Rica has a long, proud tradition of coffee production, and a fine Costa Rican coffee is the quintessential Latin-American type, perfectly balancing acidity and body. The better coffees come from the mountains facing the Pacific (to the west), rather than those facing the Atlantic.

The one country everyone associates with coffee, **Brazil**, does not produce the best, just the most. A good quality 'strictly soft' Brazilian Santos coffee has low acidity, a mild, mellow flavour, and a medium body. The name Santos comes from the port from which it is shipped; the term 'strictly soft' distinguishes it from the 'hard' iodine or medicinal taste, which is virtually undrinkable to all but the eastern Mediterranean palate. It is almost impossible to find Brazilian coffee worthy of the specialist trade, but it can play a valuable role in a blend.

By contrast, the world's second largest producer, **Colombia**, maintains a consistently high quality. The best Colombian coffees, such as the Supremos, have a fine, well-balanced acidity, and a medium body. Of the main producing areas – Medellin, Armenia and Manizales – the Medellin coffees have a marginally fuller body.

Guatemalan coffee can be wonderful, similar to a Costa

Bronze decoration, Caffè Tazza d'Oro, Rome

Rican, but with a lingering smoky flavour. **Mexican** coffees are light-bodied and very acidic, but the outsize Maragogipe bean is interesting to look at. **Nicaraguan** coffee can tend towards the metallic. Most of the countries of South America produce coffee, but rarely with the distinction and quality of Colombian coffee.

Jamaica Blue Mountain

Ethiopian Mocha Harrar Longberry

A selection of coffees from around the world

Mexican Maragogipe

*Monsooned Malabar
Mysore*

Kenya Peaberry

Yemeni Mocha

Cuban 'Sierra Del
Escambray'

Kenya 'AA'

Sumatra Mandheling

Celebes Kalossi

Puerto Rico Yauco Selecto

Colombian Medellin
Excelso

The Caribbean

The coffees of the Caribbean islands vary considerably, and in overall character have some of the general balance of Latin-American types, but with less acidity and a fuller flavour.

Jamaica Blue Mountain is one of the few specialist coffees of which almost everyone has heard. **Jamaican** beans enjoy an apparently unassailable status in the world of coffees. Its beans are certainly among the best looking, but the gradual inclusion of coffees from lower down the Blue Mountains, to meet the unquenchable demand particularly from Japan, has led to suspicions about the quality in the cup. In its purest form, however, it remains one of the great coffees, with a perfect balance of flavour and acidity, and a lingering aftertaste.

Today **Cuba** sells all its Crystal Mountain coffee from the Sierra del Escambray region to the Japanese market. Grown on soil rich with quartziferous and micaceous crystals (which are thought

Gathering coffee cherries in the West Indies, late 19th century

Recipe for Coffee Eclairs

Boil 8fl oz (250ml) of water, 3oz (75g) of butter and 2oz (50g) of sugar; quickly add 5oz (150g) of flour, whilst stirring vigorously. When it is thoroughly mixed, add four beaten eggs. Place the mixture in little elongated shapes on a preheated baking sheet greased with butter. Once the éclairs are cooked, put them to one side and fill with crème pâtissière. Put in a bain marie (water bath) fondant chocolate and two spoonfuls of very strong coffee. When the mixture has thoroughly melted, spread on top of the éclairs and allow to cool.

to encourage healthy growth in the coffee plant), the coffee has a low acidity and is delightfully smooth, with a hint of the flavour of the cedar wood used in cigar tubes.

Recent American investment has revived the **Puerto Rican** coffee industry. **Santo Domingo** occasionally produces a very pleasant batch of coffees, and Strictly High Grown coffee from **Haiti**, although erratic, sometimes has a rich soft flavour.

East Africa and Yemen

The common characteristic of East African coffees is acidity. In the case of coffees from Ruanda and Malawi, this often results in a tart, grassy flavour, whereas in Kenyan coffees this acidity produces a highly desirable sharpness of taste.

Although **Kenyan** coffees are not of a uniformly high standard, the distinctive fruity acidity (which typifies the best) is still evident, albeit only slightly, in the lower quality varieties as well. As a result, it is very difficult for a blender to find a substitute flavour from another country to make up this characteristic, and so Kenyan coffee is much in demand at all quality levels. A top-quality Kenyan coffee is amongst the best in the world, with a rich fruity acidity, unmatched by any other.

Ethiopia has successfully hijacked the term Mocha which was originally applied only to Yemeni coffees shipped from that port. Some of the Ethiopian 'washed' coffees, where the coffee cherry is soaked away from the bean using water, are sublime; Sidamo and Harrar Longberry can have wonderful blackcurrant notes to their acidity.

The coffee terraces of Yemen

Authentic **Yemeni** Mocha coffee is very hard to find these days, not least because the country has given over many of the old coffee plantations to the cultivation of Qat, a mild stimulant. The cultivation of the coffee on ancient irrigated terracing, together with the antiquated processing machinery used, makes Yemeni coffee true 'liquid history'. Wildly erratic, with spicy undertones and a wine-like acidity, Yemeni Mocha coffee is the most distinctive and elusive of the world's coffees.

Tanzania produces some rather dull coffees which are much sought-after in Japan, due apparently to the resemblance of Kilimanjaro to Mount Fuji rather than any inherent qualities. **Zambia** is a tiny producer, but nevertheless capable of producing coffees which very occasionally have a sublime oily aftertaste.

India and the Far East

Coffees from this hemisphere are generally low in acidity, heavy-bodied and smooth. However, the further out into the Pacific the coffee is grown, the more the body decreases and the acidity increases.

Koorg and Mysore provinces in southern **India** produce coffees with a pleasant mellow flavour, but without any real distinction. However, in Monsooned Malabar, a coffee produced by allowing the beans to dry in the monsoon winds, south India possesses one of the world's most evocatively named coffees.

The Blue **Sumatran** coffees, as well as those from the

Coffee estate in Ceylon, late 19th century

Mandheling area, are extraordinarily heavy-bodied, rich and smooth. Some **Javan** coffees, such as Old Brown Java, are allowed to age, which further accentuates these characteristics.

Celebes, now Sulawesi, still markets coffee under its former Dutch colonial name. Celebes Kalossi is a classic coffee, combining elements of the heavy-bodied Javan coffees with the acidity and fruitiness of Hawaiian coffee.

In **Hawaii** the renaissance of the Kona plantations, thanks to American investment, has led to one of the world's first 'designer' coffees. Well-marketed, beautifully packaged and impeccably produced, Hawaiian Kona has everything except real character. A medium-bodied, fairly acid coffee.

Recipe for Tropical Coffee Cake

Make a mixture of 2oz (50g) of flour, a cup of very strong coffee, and 2oz (50g) of caster sugar. Add a few drops of vanilla essence and enough milk so that the mixture can be rolled out as pastry without difficulty. Spread some pastry in a flan dish greased with butter. Sprinkle with a handful of grapes, seeded and soaked in rum, and then add three sliced bananas. Spread the rest of the pastry on top, and glaze with the yolk of an egg. Sprinkle with white sugar, and leave in a hot oven for half an hour. Remove and, once the cake has cooled, serve with fresh whipped cream.

Celebrated Coffee Houses

Coffee drinking has always been a social activity. Poets and story-tellers entertained the patrons of the Mecca coffee houses, while their wives complained that they spent more time in the coffee houses than at home with them. Their revenge came, however, with the passing of a law making the provision of coffee for wives part of the marriage contract.

The traditional Viennese coffee houses date from 1683, when the Turks left 500 sacks of coffee behind after abandoning the siege of the city. A Polish interpreter, Franz Georg Kolschitzky, who had carried messages across the Turkish lines in disguise, asked for the coffee as his reward, and subsequently opened the first Viennese coffee house with great success.

Café Griensteidl, Vienna, 1890

Lloyd's coffee house, 18th century

After its introduction to England in 1650, the popularity of coffee spread like wildfire, particularly in London. Some coffee houses at this time formed the starting point for institutions which are now world famous. Lloyd's, the insurance company, for example, started life at Lloyd's coffee house. Jonathan's, in Change Alley, became the Stock Exchange and the messengers on the dealing floor were still known as 'waiters' until its closure recently. For a hundred years the London coffee houses maintained a tradition of freedom of speech and thought. The social elite could sit down with poets, merchants and tinkers, and exchange opinions over a cup of coffee. For this reason they became known as 'Penny Universities' – a penny being the price of the coffee.

A Question of Taste

*E*very country has its own way of brewing coffee, and the gadgets to make it vary from the simplicity of the *ibrik*, to the technical complexity of an espresso machine.

Coffee should be ground according to the brewing method that will be used. The best coffee grinders are properly constructed to grind the coffee between rollers (operated by hand or by electricity), which open up the cell structure of the bean to allow the full flavour to be released. Most home food processors have a grinding attachment which smashes the beans with its blades. This is not the ideal method, but is relatively quick and effective. To truly pulverize coffee for brewing in an *ibrik*, a mortar and pestle should be used.

Coffee grinder

The United States

America is the biggest consumer of coffee worldwide. The endless refill cups of coffee in restaurants and diners, brewed in bulk by filter, tend to be rather weak and lacking in character, and a recent reaction to this is the current fashion for espresso coffee and the boom in gourmet coffees. These fine quality coffees have restored coffee to its rightful place as an interesting, diverse beverage. Flavoured coffees are also very popular, with varieties such as Amaretto, Chocolate Mint and Orange coffees widely available. Iced coffee, as well as a wide selection of decaffeinated coffees, complete the picture of America as one of the most exciting places for a coffee lover to visit.

Northern Europe

In Finland they prefer classic filter coffee to any other. This method is widely used in the Western world, and has the advantage of producing a clear cup of coffee, free from any suspended grounds. Automatic electric filter machines are very convenient, but if the coffee is kept on the hot plate any longer than half an hour, it starts to deteriorate, acquiring a rather bitter flavour.

The playwright Christopher Fry claimed 'Coffee in England is just toasted milk.'

Greece, Turkey and the Middle East

These countries use the *ibrik* – a brass or enamel vessel with
a narrow neck and a long handle, which is placed directly
over the heat. The coffee is ground as fine as possible, and a
tablespoonful is stirred into cold water with a little sugar in
the *ibrik*. This is then placed on the heat,
and as it comes to the boil and froths up
the neck, it is removed, allowed to cool
for a moment, and then
boiled again. This is
repeated three times,

*Middle Eastern coffee
pots and cups*

and the coffee has a fine froth when poured into small cups. The fine grounds settle to the bottom. In some countries cardamom seeds or ground ginger are added for extra flavour. This is probably the oldest way of brewing coffee, and is best made with a genuine Yemeni Mocha; in Greece and Turkey, however, a 'hard' Brazilian or Rioy coffee is often used instead.

Recipe for Crème Pâtissière au Café

Mix 3 whole eggs with 6oz (175g) of caster sugar and 2½oz (65g) of flour. Once it is all thoroughly mixed, add to 8fl oz (250ml) of milk and the same amount of sweet strong coffee in a saucepan which has already cooled. Stir well, and continue to stir whilst heating it for a few minutes.

Egyptian palace, early 19th century

The Revolutionary Drink

Coffee's reputation as a mild stimulant has long attracted the attention of those of a zealous and serious disposition. First into the fray was Kair Bey, the 16th century Governor of Mecca, who banned the drinking of coffee, and coffee houses themselves, believing them to inspire such irreverent activities as singing and dancing. Unfortunately he proudly reported his ban to the Sultan of Cairo, where coffee was all the rage, who promptly rescinded the order. Kair Bey was beheaded shortly afterwards.

The next attempt to prohibit coffee was made by the Turks, with first Suleyman the Magnificent, and later Kuprili, Grand Vizier of Constantinople, banning its consumption. Suspecting coffee houses to be a hotbed of sedition, Kuprili ordered that anyone caught drinking coffee should be tied into a sack and thrown into the Bosphorus. His opinion was shared by Charles II of England, who banned coffee for the stimulating intellectual conversations it provoked. Later the Storming of the Bastille, the first act of the French Revolution, was rumoured to have started in a coffee house near the opera, and the Green Dragon coffee house in Boston was a regular meeting place for the architects of the American War of Independence.

Moorish coffee shop, 1903

France

France's historical relationship with coffee is complex; Napoleon tried to bypass the effects of the British blockade by recommending that the French use chicory as a coffee substitute, a habit which remained long after the blockade was lifted. More recently, after colonizing West Africa, the French took over its plantations, where inferior robusta coffee varieties are grown, only to find themselves having to go to great lengths to try to disguise the flavour. In contemporary France, espresso coffee is now the most popular; the morning café crème is a sumptuous brew of espresso topped with warm milk, tailor-made for the dunking of croissants.

Despite its French-sounding name, the cafetière – a glass or steel pot with a plunger which forces the separation of the grounds and the coffee – is actually used less in France than in countries such as Britain. It is nonetheless a very satisfactory way of making coffee, which has the simple virtues of the basic jug method – whereby boiling water is poured onto coffee in a jug, stirred and then poured – but avoids the problem of grounds floating in the coffee.

Recipe for Coffee Cream Horns

Prepare a sweet dry pastry with 7oz (200g) of flour, 3oz (75g) of caster sugar, 3oz (75g) of butter and one egg. Put the pastry in horn moulds, making sure that it is spread evenly.

In the meantime, make a mixture of 2½oz (65g) of sugar, 3 whole eggs, 2oz (50g) of powdered almonds and ¼ pint (250ml) of strong coffee and put it in the horns. Cook for a quarter of an hour.

Napoleon's Coffee

Concerned that the stranglehold of Mocha on the coffee trade was not to their advantage, the East India Company decided to experiment with growing coffee on their island of St Helena in the South Atlantic. A Company agent was sent from Mocha to buy coffee seeds at the market of Bait Al-Faqih, in the foothills of the mountains where the coffee was grown. The first seeds arrived on the island in 1732. Although commercial production never really took off, by the time that Napoleon was incarcerated there after the Battle of Waterloo, there was enough growing on the island to supply its needs. Napoleon hated the island, and is rumoured to have complained that the only good thing about it was the coffee. As he lay dying in 1821, his loyal aide Marshal Bertrand recalled: 'Tears came to my eyes at the sight of the this man who has inspired such awe…pleading now for a little spoonful of coffee, begging permission like a child. Although evidently good enough to make an emperor weep, and later to win a Gold Medal at the Great Exhibition of 1851, St Helena coffee has now sunk into relative obscurity, although the descendants of those selfsame seeds from Mocha still grow on the island today.

A New Mapp of the Island of
SAINT HELLENA
By Sam Thornton Hydrographer at the
Sign of England Scotland and Ireland in
the Minories London

Italy

The favourite of Italians – although the prototype machine was invented in England and the name derives from the French – espresso coffee has become hugely, and internationally, popular. Its secret lies in its fast high-pressure but low-temperature extraction, which draws the flavours out of a coffee without burning it. Enthusiasts swear this method produces the best cup of coffee, but it requires a particular

1950s espresso machine

kind of blend, and does not work well with pure specialist coffees, such as those from Kenya or Costa Rica. It is also virtually impossible to create the required pressure in a domestic espresso machine, and so the flavour of an espresso produced on a full-specification professional machine will always be difficult to reproduce at home. But when an espresso coffee is good, it is very, very good.

Espresso Recipes

Espresso A single demitasse of espresso coffee, black, usually drunk with sugar. Can be flavoured with a drop or two of almond or tangerine extract.

Espresso Ristretto Diluted with less water to produce a very strong espresso.

Espresso Romano A demitasse of espresso served with a thin slice of lemon on the side. Popular in the United States.

Double or Doppio A full 6fl oz (175ml) cup of straight espresso. For the professional.

Cappuccino (French: café crème) About one-third espresso, one-third hot milk, topped with one-third foam, in a heavy cup. Like the others, often drunk with sugar. The foam of the cappuccino, and of caffè latte, may be garnished with a dash of unsweetened cocoa or cinnamon.

Caffè Latte (French: café au lait; Spanish: cafe con leche) One or two shots of espresso, and about three times that amount of foamed milk in a large bowl or wide-mouthed glass. The favourite breakfast drink of southern Europeans. Caffè latte has a greater proportion of milk to coffee than a cappuccino, and tastes weaker and milkier. Strictly speaking, the milk and coffee should be poured simultaneously, one from either side of the bowl.

Coretto Espresso which has been 'corrected' with a dash of amoretto, sambucco or grappa.

Espresso Macchiato A demitasse of espresso 'marked' with a dab of hot, foamed milk.

Espresso Con Panna As above, with whipped cream.

Latte Macchiato In terms of presentation, a classic. An 8fl oz or ½ pint (250 or 300ml) glass half-filled with hot, foamed milk, into which a demitasse of espresso is slowly dribbled. The coffee colours the milk darker at the top, shading to a light brown at the bottom, then a contrasting layer of pure white foam is added to the top. Flaked chocolate is sprinkled on last.

Mocha The name of this most well known coffee takes on a special meaning for an espresso lover. About one-third espresso, one-third strong, unsweetened hot chocolate, and one-third steamed milk. The milk goes in last, and it is usually served in a mug.

Decaffeinated and instant

Caffeine is a white alkaloid substance which is a diuretic and can cause palpitations when taken in large doses. It comprises around three per cent of the total weight of a coffee bean and is not destroyed in roasting. By a quirk of nature, high quality arabica coffees have about half the caffeine content of poor quality robustas, so the first step for those wishing to reduce their caffeine intake is simply to drink better coffee. Failing that, an alternative method is to drink decaffeinated coffee, which has had the caffeine removed from the beans before roasting.

Despite the best efforts of the coffee industry, and a bewildering array of methods for extracting the caffeine, it is still not possible to do so without damaging the flavour.

The coffee industry also invests vast amounts of money each year in pursuit of its ultimate goal – an instant coffee

which tastes as good as the real thing. Although the quality has improved substantially over the years, an instant coffee has yet to be produced that can replace the aroma, body and flavour of a freshly roasted, freshly made cup of fine coffee.

Dr Oliver Wendell Holmes, the American writer and physician, noted, 'The morning cup of coffee has an exhilaration about it which the cheering influence of the afternoon or evening cup of tea cannot be expected to reproduce.'

Index

Picture Credits

The publisher thanks the photographers and organisations for their kind
permission to reproduce the following photographs in this book:

Collection Marques de Villamizar/Bridgeman Art Library,
jacket photograph;

Christie's Images 1, 52–53;
Kupperstichkabinett, Berlin/Bridgeman Art Library 2–3;
Mary Evans Picture Library 7, 27, 62;
The Robert Opie Collection 8;
The Stapleton Collection 10–11, 51;
Jean-Loup Charmet 12, 16–17, 19, 20;
Michael Holford 14–15;
Antony Wild 21, 40;
The Edward Bramah Tea and Coffee Museum 26, 47–49, 54, 58;
Museo Nacional Bellas Artes, Rio de Janeiro/Index/
Bridgeman Art Library 22–23;
Hutchison Library 24;
Musée de la Ville de Paris, Maison de Balzac/Lauros-Giraudon 29;
Hulton Deutsch 31, 46;
The Advertising Archives 32, 61;
Francesco Venturi 35;
Theo Bergström 36–37;
Ann Ronan/Image Select 38, 42;
Stadtische Museum, Vienna/Bridgeman Art Library 44–45;
Bodum 55;
New York Public Library 56–57.

The publisher has tried its utmost to clear copyright with
all the relevant copyright holders but if there are any additions
it will be pleased to add them.